34134 00251785 9

Leabharlainn nan Eilean Siar

WITHDRAWN

D0655886

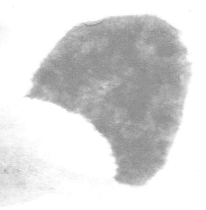

BEGINNING HISTORY

GREEK CITIES

WESTERN ISLES
LIBRARIES
31200
WITHDRAWN

Barry Steel

Illustrated by Bernard Long

Wayland

BEGINNING HISTORY

Crusaders
Egyptian Pyramids
Greek Cities
Medieval Markets
Norman Castles
Roman Soldiers
Saxon Villages
Tudor Sailors
Victorian Children
Viking Explorers

All words that appear in **bold** are explained in the glossary on page 22.

Series editor: Catherine Ellis
Book editor: Penny Horton
Designer: Helen White

First published in 1989 by Wayland (Publishers) Limited, 61 Western Road, Hove, East Sussex, BN3 1JD.

© Copyright 1989 Wayland (Publishers) Ltd

British Library Cataloguing in Publication Data
Steel, Barry
Greek cities
1. Greece. Cities. Social life. Friendship, ancient period
I. Title   II. Series
938′.06

ISBN 1–85210–778–2

Typeset by Kalligraphics Limited, Horley, Surrey.
Printed in Italy by G. Canale & C.S.p.A., Turin.
Bound in Belgium by Casterman, S.A.

CONTENTS

CITY STATES

Ancient Greek cities were much smaller than those of today, but each one was run like a small country, with everything it needed, including its own government, laws, army and money. Some cities were ruled by kings, while others were run by a small group of powerful men. In cities such as Athens, all men could vote to make decisions about how their city should be run.

In many ways the main Greek

cities, such as Athens, Sparta, Corinth, Delphi, Olympia, Argos and others, were alike. The language, and the religion were the same, and life in all the cities was fairly similar.

Cities often fought wars against each other, so a strong, high wall was built all the way round each city to keep attackers out. Inside the city wall was a fort called the **acropolis**, built on top of a hill. The houses were built close together and most of the streets were narrow, shady and steep. They were dusty in dry weather and muddy when it rained.

THE AGORA

The heart of the city was a large open space called the **agora**. This was the main meeting place and market. From sunrise to sunset the agora was filled with crowds of people meeting friends and doing their shopping. Many people also came here to get water from the public fountain house and to buy slaves from the slave traders.

A slave being sold in the agora.

Left The ruins of the agora at Athens as they look today.

Below A ruined statue in the agora at Athens.

If an important decision had to be made, the government would call all the **citizens** to the agora to vote.

All around the agora were **colonnades** called stoas and behind these were splendid and important stone and marble public buildings. There were law courts where criminals were tried and a **council chamber** where the city council met, as well as shops and offices. The main temples were placed near the agora.

MARKETS AND SHOPS

Most shopping was done in and around the agora. There were market stalls in the open space, selling food, clothes and goods for people's everyday needs. The crowds of shoppers were always eager for a bargain and argued fiercely over prices. Sometimes there would be a conjurer, acrobats or a juggler to entertain them. Most of the shoppers

The ruins of the Acropolis at Athens.

were men and many were **slaves**. The women usually stayed at home.

The shops in the buildings around the agora were very small and each sold only one kind of product. Usually the shopkeeper selling the goods had made them himself. To control the prices of these goods, the city's government paid men to make sure that shopkeepers did not charge too much, and to check that their scales and measures were correct.

Shopping in the agora. A fruit seller argues about prices with a customer. In the background a juggler entertains shoppers.

HOUSES

A wealthy Greek family might have lived in a house like the one in the picture. The rooms were built around a courtyard and most of the doors and windows opened into the yard to keep out the noise, smell and heat of the streets. Larger houses had an upstairs floor with bedrooms and a living area for the family's slaves. There were separate living and dining rooms for men and women, and a kitchen and bathroom with a

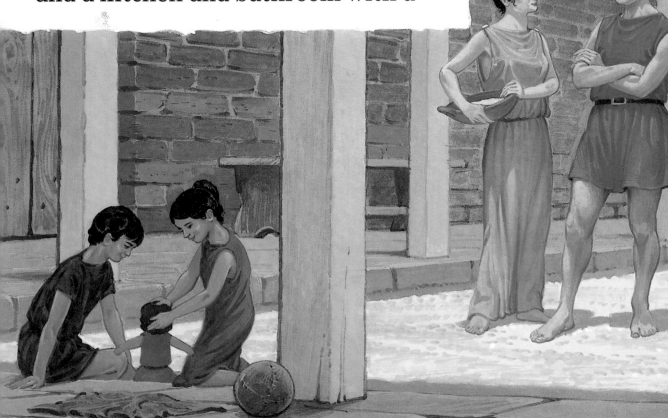

drain that led to an open gutter in the street. A well in the courtyard supplied these wealthy homes with fresh water.

Poor families had to live, eat, sleep and cook in one or two rooms and fetch their water from the public fountain house in the agora. Both rich and poor threw their rubbish into the streets.

All houses were built with soft mud bricks and had tiled roofs. Most had beaten earth floors, although the houses of some of the wealthier citizens would have had stone floors.

HOME LIFE

The inside of a Greek family's house would seem bare and uncomfortable to us. The floors had no carpets and light came from oil lamps and heat from charcoal **braziers**, so the rooms were very smoky. Furniture was made of wood and had little padding. There were no cupboards or drawers. Many items were simply hung on nails in the walls, and larger objects were kept in wooden chests.

A poor family sit down for their evening meal.

Left A painting on a Greek vase. A rich girl is decorated with jewellery before her wedding.

Greek men spent little time at home during the day, while the women hardly ever went out. The mistress of the house spent her time organizing the cooking, weaving and cleaning, with the help of slaves.

The main family meal was in the evening. For the poor, this might have been porridge or bread made from barley, sometimes with fruit, cheese or vegetables, with water or goat's milk to drink. Rich families could afford wheat bread and cakes and they drank wine with their meals. Meat was only eaten, even by the rich, at special festivals.

Below Rich homes were decorated with beautiful statues and paintings.

SCHOOLS

Above A painting on a Greek vase showing young people dancing to the music of a flute.

In Ancient Greece, only the boys went to school. They began when they were six and left at fourteen or fifteen. They were taken by a slave who would stay with them all day. Schools were usually just one room with no desks or chairs, and some schools were held in the open air. All the teachers were men and they were very strict. They taught the boys to count on an **abacus**, as well as reading and writing, music, dancing and poetry. The pupils wrote with a

Right A Greek statue of children playing knucklebones, a game similar to 'jacks'.

14

pointed stick on a **wax tablet**. The other end of the stick, which was flat, was used for rubbing out.

Girls stayed at home and learned cooking, sewing and other household skills by watching and helping their mothers. In richer families they were taught to read, write and count, usually by a slave.

Toys were very simple. Children had hoops, dolls made of wood or wax and balls made of leather.

Greek boys at work in their open-air school.

TEMPLES

The Greeks believed in many gods and goddesses. Each one looked after a particular part of life. There was Athena, goddess of wisdom; Poseidon, god of the sea; Aphrodite, goddess of love; Ares, god of war, and many others. Zeus was ruler of all the gods. Every Greek city had temples for the main gods and goddesses with an especially large and beautiful one for the particular god or goddess who protected the city.

In the centre of the temple was a large, dimly-lit room called the cella. Inside this room was a statue of the god or goddess of each temple, and a table where people could place gifts. The roof rested on the high, thick walls of the cella and was held up by many columns.

When people needed help from a god or goddess, they would kill an animal at an altar outside the temple and offer it as a gift. The Ancient Greeks believed that this would please the god or goddess and so their prayers would be answered.

THE THEATRE

A large audience enjoying a play in a Greek theatre. The chorus stand in the circular space with the main actors on the stage behind.

Plays were put on at Greek theatres on only a few special days during the year, as part of religious festivals. Prices were very low, and nearly everyone wanted to enjoy this special treat, so theatres were very large. The audience sat on rows of seats cut out of a hillside. The main actors performed on a stage called the proskenion. Between this and the

Left A vase painting showing a scene from a Greek comedy. An old man is climbing a ladder to offer a gift of apples to the young woman at the window.

audience was a circular space called the orchestra, where the **chorus** sang, spoke and danced.

Because the theatre was so large, it was difficult to see the actors' faces, so they wore large masks to show what kind of character they were playing. A visit to the theatre lasted all day and the audience would see several plays — sad, serious plays called tragedies; amusing plays called comedies; and lastly, a very funny play to send people home with smiling faces.

Below Actors in Greek plays wore masks like these.

SPORTS

A fit, healthy body was important to the Greeks and most men and boys made regular visits to the gymnasium. The palaestra, a large rectangular space, was used to practise running, jumping, throwing the **javelin** and **discus**, wrestling and boxing. Around the palaestra were practise rooms, changing rooms, baths and **anointing** rooms. After exercise, the athletes covered their bodies with oil and then scraped themselves clean.

Athletic contests were held in the town's **stadium**. This had a long running track with rows of seats along the sides and at one end.

No clothes were worn in the gymnasium and the stadium, so women and girls were not allowed in.

All the main cities held sports contests as part of their religious festivals. The most famous was the Olympic Games, held every four years at the city of Olympia. Of course, we still have the Olympic Games – one of the many ideas handed down to us by the Ancient Greeks.

GLOSSARY

Abacus A wooden frame with strings of beads that can be used for counting.

Acropolis The place where people would have sheltered if their city was attacked.

Agora A large open space. The main market and meeting place of an Ancient Greek city.

Anointing Covering the body with oil.

Brazier A metal container in which charcoal is burned to give heat.

Chorus A group of people who sang, danced and helped to tell the story in Greek plays.

Citizens The people who live in a city and have the right to vote.

Colonnades A row of evenly-spaced columns holding up a roof over a path.

Council Chamber A room where the council, a group of people who make decisions about the government of a city, meet.

Discus A flat, heavy circle of wood or metal. People compete to see who can throw it the farthest.

Javelin A long, light spear. People compete to see who can throw it the farthest.

Slaves People who are owned by another person and are not free.

Stadium A course for races. In Ancient Greece it was usually between two hills which provided slopes for rows of seats.

Wax Tablet A wooden board covered in soft wax used for writing.

BOOKS TO READ.

Alexander the Great and the Greeks by Nathaniel Harris (Wayland, 1985).

Ancient Greece by Anne Millard (Usborne, 1981).

The Greeks by Judith Crosher (Macdonald, 1974).

The Greeks by Anne and Barry Steel (Wayland, 1986).

Growing Up in Ancient Greece by Amanda Purves (Wayland, 1978).

See Inside an Ancient Greek Town by Jonathan Rutland (Kingfisher, 1986).

A Slave in Ancient Greece by Miriam Moss (Wayland, 1986).

Picture Acknowledgements

The publishers would like to thank the following for providing the photographs in this book: Mary Evans Picture Library 13, 19; Michael Holford 13, 14, 19; Werner Forman Archive Ltd 14; Zefa 7 (top and bottom), 8. All the illustrations were provided by Bernard Long.

INDEX